Wonderful Wellbeing

Becky Dickinson

Illustrated by **Masha Ukhova**

OXFORD
UNIVERSITY PRESS

Letter from the Author

I hope you enjoy this book on wellbeing. More importantly, I hope it inspires you to look after your mind and body.

One of the reasons I love writing books is that I'm always learning new things from my research. I can't wait to start using some of the ideas I discovered when researching this book, including starting a gratitude journal and trying to be kind every day.

One of my favourite ways to look after myself is to spend time outdoors. I love going for walks with my dog and three children, and spending time near the sea where I live. I'm trying to learn to surf, although it's quite challenging and I often end up in the water! I also enjoy gardening and growing vegetables.

Try to take care of your own wellbeing by finding ways to relax and have fun. I wish you all health and happiness.

Becky Dickinson

Contents

What is Wellbeing?..4

Be Good to Your Body..14

Be Kind to Your Mind...24

Be Good to Others...32

Glossary...39

Index...40

The glossary

Some words in this book are in **bold**. When you read a **bold** word, think about what it means. If you don't know, you can look it up in the glossary at the end of the book.

What is Wellbeing?

We often think that being healthy, or feeling well, means not having any illnesses or injuries, such as a broken leg or a virus. People usually know how to help keep their bodies healthy, by exercising and eating the right kinds of foods. All of this results in good physical health. This is an important aspect of feeling well, but it's not the only one.

Being healthy also includes the way you think and how you're feeling: your mental wellbeing. You can't see it because it's inside your head, but that doesn't mean it's not real.

Feeling well on the inside and on the outside can help us to feel positive, get on with others, have fun and cope with difficulties.

wellbeing: the state of being comfortable, healthy or happy

Good wellbeing doesn't mean you feel fantastic all the time, but it does give you the resilience to deal with life's ups and downs.

People who are resilient are good at facing challenges and overcoming difficulties. Whether it's learning how to solve tricky maths questions, changing schools or coping with a **pandemic**, they find a way to 'bounce back' from problems.

resilience: the capacity to recover quickly from difficulties

Understanding Emotions

Which of these words would you use to describe how you feel today? Pick three words from this page, or write down three of your own.

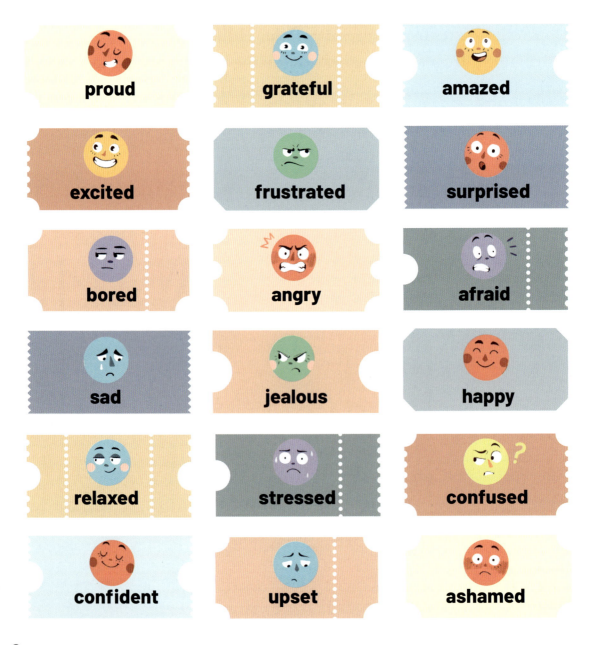

Feelings play a big role in our lives; they are part of being human. Feelings cover a range of emotions, from happiness and excitement to anger and sadness. All emotions are important, even the ones you don't like very much. That means you shouldn't ignore them!

Feelings can change more quickly than you can change your socks! Don't worry, that's normal too.

It's important to recognize when you are worried or unhappy so that you can work out why you feel that way, and can find a solution. Just like feeling thirsty tells you it's time to drink something, feeling an emotion can tell you it's time to solve a problem.

I feel *ashamed* that I shouted at my sister.

I should say sorry to her.

I'm *angry* there's so much plastic in the sea.

I'll make a difference by using less plastic and recycling more.

I'm *sad* that my friends are leaving me out.

I'll try talking to them about how their actions make me feel.

Worries and difficulties are part of growing up, but some feelings can weigh us down.

Other feelings can help keep life in balance.

Scientists have shown that our brains pay more attention to difficult emotions and experiences than happier ones. This means we are more likely to remember when someone is mean to us than when they are kind. But by training our brains to notice more of the good things, we can change the way we think and feel, too.

The Power of Positivity

Psychologists from the University of North Carolina have shown that developing a positive attitude can enable us to overcome problems and build new skills. Here are some scientifically proven ways to help you think more positively and feel fantastic.

Be helpful

You could offer to take a neighbour's dog for a walk, help a younger child with their reading or do something useful in your community, such as litter picking. Helping others means you will feel more connected with the people around you, which is a great way to enhance your wellbeing.

Try a new activity

Your confidence will grow if you set yourself goals – and you'll get a sense of achievement from working towards your goals, too. You could try a new sport or teach yourself a skill such as origami, chess or coding.

Make 'yet' your favourite word

Change 'I can't do it' to 'I can't do it *yet*.' Your abilities aren't fixed, which means you can get better at something if you set your mind to it and don't give up. This attitude is called having a growth mindset. People who have a growth mindset believe they can get better at something with practice, so they find ways to overcome setbacks and challenges.

Feeling Grateful

Gratitude is another positive quality. It means being thankful for what we have, such as our homes and families, and paying attention to all the little things that make us smile, such as a beautiful sunny day or a glittering night sky.

Try this: each day, think of three things you are grateful for. Write them down on a piece of paper and keep them in a special jar, or you could make a 'gratitude journal' and record them there. If you have a bad day, look over your gratitude notes to lift your mood.

Dr Robert A Emmons, a psychologist from the University of California, is a world expert on the subject of gratitude. His studies have shown that people who feel grateful for what they have are happier and healthier than people who don't.

Can you think of a time when you said thank you, not just to be polite, but because you really meant it? Ask yourself:

- When was the last time I felt truly thankful?
- What happened?
- How did it make me feel inside?
- Could I put that feeling of gratitude to good use by helping someone else?

Feeling grateful for the support we receive, and remembering the difference it makes, can inspire us to give our support to others, too.

Remember: people don't always feel able to ask for help, so noticing when they need support can make the biggest difference of all.

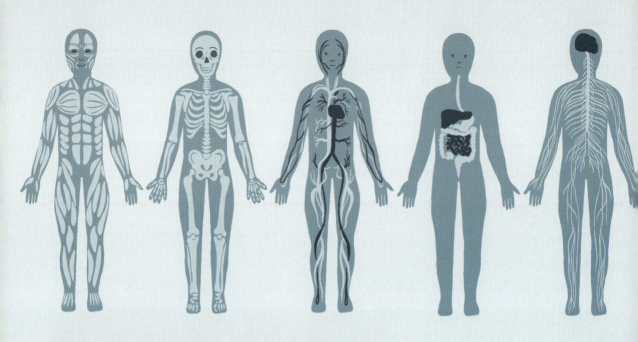

Be Good to Your Body

Bodies come in all different shapes and sizes. While we don't all look the same on the outside, our bodies work the same way on the inside.

By the time you are an adult you will have 60 000 miles of blood vessels inside your body – enough to stretch nearly two and half times around the Earth!

Your bones are constantly supporting you and are stronger than concrete.

Your brain produces enough electricity to power a small light bulb.

Your eyes blink around 20 times a minute. That's between 5.2 million and 7.1 million blinks a year!

Your lungs take between 17 000 and 29 000 breaths a day.

When your heart is resting it beats between 86 000 and 144 000 times a day.

Scientists believe that the body replaces most skin cells around every month. They are made deep in the skin, and are pushed towards the surface where they replace old cells.

Time to Move

Did you know that being active can improve your mood, too?

- When you notice your body getting fitter or stronger, your self-esteem may get a boost. This can mean that you will feel more confident in yourself and your abilities.
- Taking part in sport can be a good way of setting yourself goals to achieve. Working as part of a team makes us feel good, too.
- When you are active, your brain pumps out special 'happiness' chemicals called endorphins. Endorphins make you feel more positive.

Playing sport isn't the only way to be active. We can look after our bodies in our daily lives, too. Here are some active ideas:

- Walk, cycle or scoot to school if possible.
- Get off the bus one stop earlier, or ask whoever's driving you to park further away so that you walk further.
- Play with a ball, skipping rope or hula hoop.
- Try an online workout. Lots of experts and coaches have made videos that are free to access.
- Play in the park.
- Go for a walk, swim or bike ride with friends or family.

Online workouts make training more **accessible**, and they can often be done even in small spaces.

Time for Bed

After all that activity, you'll need to get some rest. Do any of these sound familiar?

> I'm not tired.

> Can't I stay up later tonight?

> It's too early to go to bed.

You might not always feel like going to bed, but all living creatures need rest.

Newborn babies generally sleep for up to 17 hours a day because they are growing and developing at such a rapid rate. Although you are not growing as quickly as you did when you were first born, sleep is incredibly important for children (and adults) of all ages.

If you are between 7 and 12 years old, you need about 10 to 11 hours of sleep each night.

When we don't get enough sleep, we struggle to concentrate. Sleep allows your body and brain to rest and recover, so you feel alert and full of energy the next day. It also strengthens your **immune system**, which helps your body fight infection and keeps you healthy.

Sleep can benefit learning, too. During the day, your brain cells form connections with other parts of the brain as you are learning. Scientists think that during the night, the important connections are made stronger while the less important ones are deleted.

We spend around a third of our lives sleeping.

Sleep is made up of five different stages and together they make one sleep cycle.

Stage 1
You start to feel drowsy but can still be woken up easily.

Stage 2
After a few minutes, you fall into a slightly deeper sleep. Your brain tells your muscles to relax. Your heart rate and breathing slow down. Your body temperature drops slightly.

Stage 3
Now you are deeply asleep. Your brain waves, which reflect the activity of your brain, slow down. Some people sleepwalk or talk in their sleep during this stage.

Stage 4
This is the deepest sleep of all. If you are woken up, you'll feel confused for a few minutes. We need the deep sleep of stages 3 and 4 to feel refreshed in the morning. Sleepwalking can occur during this stage, too.

Stage 5
After the first four stages of sleep, you enter **REM** sleep, which stands for rapid eye movement. This is when most dreams occur and our eyes dart around beneath the eyelids. REM sleep usually occurs around 90 minutes into the sleep cycle.

Sleepy Animal Facts

- Some species of birds, such as the great frigatebird, sleep in mid-air. This allows them to fly vast distances over the sea.

- Some animals, such as giraffes and zebras, can sleep standing up so they are less **vulnerable** to predators.

- **Herbivores** tend to sleep for less time than **carnivores**. This is because their food contains less energy, so they need to spend more time eating in order to get the energy they need. Carnivores are more likely to get their energy from one large meal.

Our Internal Clock

We all have a 'clock' in our brains which tells us when to sleep and when to wake up. This cycle is called your circadian (*say* sur-kay-dee-an) rhythm. Here are some tips to help it run smoothly.

Stick to a routine

Going to bed and getting up around the same time every day keeps your body clock in a regular pattern which helps you to fall asleep easily and quickly.

Swap your drink

Drinks containing too much sugar can keep you awake. Try to avoid these in the afternoon and evening, and drink water instead.

Tidy up

A disorganized space can make it harder to fall asleep. Tidy the room for a better night's sleep.

Switch off screens

Electronic devices like mobile phones release blue light that can stop your body producing melatonin, a **hormone** that makes us feel drowsy. Turning off screens at least an hour before bed helps prepare your brain for sleep.

Run around (but not before bedtime)

Being energetic means you are more likely to feel tired in the evening. It's best not to exercise too late though, as this can make you more alert when it's time to relax.

Time to Eat

Eating a balanced diet gives us the energy and nutrients we need to grow, play and learn. Different foods have different benefits, so we need to eat a wide variety to give our body everything it needs.

Carbohydrates provide the energy you need to run and play without getting tired.

Fruit and vegetables contain fibre and important vitamins and minerals that help to keep our bodies healthy. Try to eat at least five portions of fruit and vegetables every day.

Your body is around two-thirds water and we all need to keep hydrated to stay healthy. Children need to drink about one litre of fluid a day, so always keep a bottle of water nearby.

Protein is used by your body to repair muscle and make new cells.

Fats and oils also give us energy, but we only need small amounts of these.

Dairy products contain calcium that helps keep our bones strong. If you don't eat dairy, you can find calcium in other foods including some nuts, seeds and bony fish.

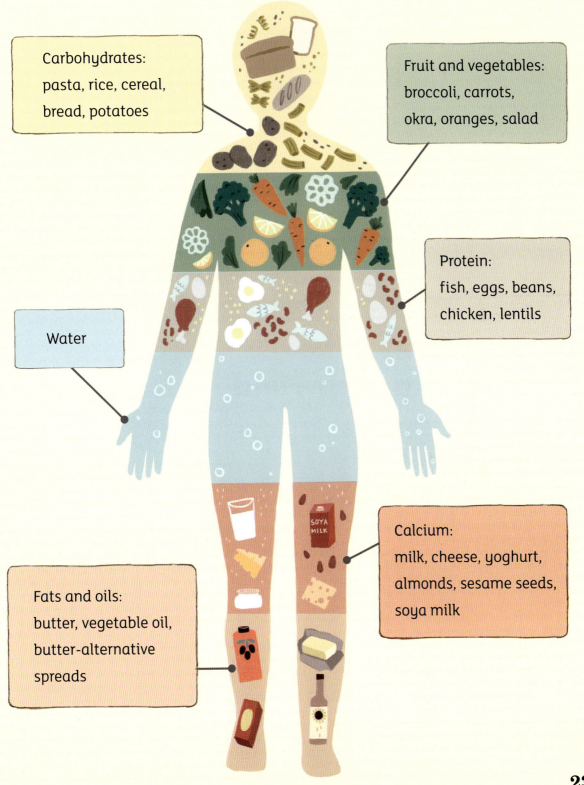

Be Kind to Your Mind

Mental wellbeing is a term you may have heard of, but might not always understand.

Your mental wellbeing is about the way you feel, and how well you cope with daily life and any challenges you face.

We all have days when we feel sad, angry, or worried. Most of the time, these feelings don't last too long, but when they do, our mental wellbeing can suffer. This can make it harder to cope with difficult situations. Just as we can be kind to our bodies by eating healthily and staying active, we can be kind to our minds as well. Our mental wellbeing influences how we think and behave, so it is important to take care of it.

Good mental wellbeing can help you to:

- recognize and express your emotions
- feel confident in your abilities and respect yourself
- get on well with others
- enjoy yourself
- cope with change and difficulties.

Here are some ways you can be kind to your mind.

Crying is good for you

When you shed tears, your body releases chemicals that make you feel better and reduce pain and stress. Crying also shows other people that you are distressed and need support.

Humans are the only animals that cry tears.

Get outdoors

Sunlight causes your brain to release a hormone called serotonin, which can improve your mood. Getting outside is a great way to improve your mental wellbeing. (Don't forget to use sunscreen whenever you spend time outside!) If you can't get outdoors, opening blinds and curtains can also make a difference to how you feel.

Spend time with people who make you happy

Being with people who make us feel happy or safe is very important for our mental wellbeing. Sharing your favourite activities with those you care about helps to strengthen these relationships.

Fight or flight

When you feel stressed or afraid, a hormone called **adrenalin** is released into your blood to help you confront challenges. This is known as the 'fight or flight' response because it enables you to react quickly.

Thousands of years ago, this reaction kept our ancestors safe by preparing them to fight, or escape (take flight) from wild animals.

Adrenalin can be useful, but sometimes our brains produce adrenalin when we don't need it. This might happen if there's a situation you don't feel comfortable with, such as spending a night away from home or meeting new people.

Too much adrenalin can make you feel nervous or anxious. You could experience some of these physical feelings too:

- panic or dizziness
- stomach ache
- racing heart
- sweaty palms
- fast breathing

Our brains are very powerful, and we can experience unpleasant physical symptoms when our mental wellbeing is suffering. This is why it's so important to look after our mental health as much as our physical health.

If you often feel nervous or anxious and you experience unpleasant physical symptoms, you should tell an adult.

What to do about worries

We all have worries, but your wellbeing can suffer when they won't go away. You might have difficulty sleeping or concentrating, or want to avoid certain situations or people. If so, it's important to develop ways to keep your worries under control. These techniques can help you to stay calm.

I'm worried I won't pass my end of year exams.

Breathe in slowly and deeply through your nose, then breathe out slowly through your mouth. This can help slow down your heart rate and your breathing, both of which can make you feel calmer.

It's important to tell a grown-up whenever you have a worry that feels too big for you to deal with on your own. Always ask for support or share your concerns if something is bothering you, especially if you are worried about your safety or the **welfare** of someone you know.

I'm starting a new school and am nervous about making new friends.

Whatever you are worried about, share your feelings with a trusted adult, such as a family member, friend, teacher or counsellor. Talking about worries can make them seem more manageable.

I can't stop thinking about whether we'll have enough money now Mum's lost her job.

When negative thoughts and feelings are trapped inside your head, it can be hard to think clearly. Write them down or draw a picture of what is worrying you. Expressing those feelings in words or pictures can help you to make sense of them.

Distracting yourself by doing something creative is a great way to help you feel less worried. You could try writing, drawing, singing, dancing around the room, playing an instrument or making models.

Be Good to Others

kindness: the quality of being friendly, generous and considerate

Studies show that when you do something nice for someone else, you get the same 'happiness chemicals' that you get from exercising. These are the hormones called endorphins. In other words, you can brighten someone else's day and your own at the same time.

There are thousands of ways to show kindness. You could lend a helping hand by opening a door, carrying a heavy bag or encouraging a classmate who's struggling with their work. How many kind acts can you carry out this week?

Develop Empathy

Empathy means understanding and sharing other people's feelings by seeing the world through their eyes. We sometimes call this 'standing in someone else's shoes'.

A great way to develop empathy is to read stories and imagine how you would react to the situations different characters find themselves in. Another way is to take an interest in people who are from different backgrounds and cultures to your own and listen to their points of view.

Empathy doesn't just change the way we feel towards other people. It can change the way we act, too …

Empathy may help us to notice opportunities to help other people. Imagine a new boy has joined your school. At lunchtime, you notice he is sitting on his own. How do you think he is feeling?

Picture yourself in the new boy's shoes. Now imagine how you would feel if someone asked you to sit at their table, or join in a game with them and their friends.

If you feel empathy and then act kindly by helping the new boy settle in, you'll end up feeling good about yourself, too.

Here are some ideas to cheer up someone else's day:

- Let someone go in front of you in a queue.
- Volunteer your time or skills at a charity event like a cake sale.
- Sort out your toys and give any you no longer play with to charity.
- Leave a surprise note for someone.
- Tell someone how much they mean to you.
- Share your games or books with a friend who might also enjoy them.

Showing Appreciation for Others

When **Covid-19** spread around the world, it made life very hard, but we learned to appreciate the people who help us more. Nurses, doctors, paramedics, carers, refuse collectors, delivery drivers and supermarket workers carried on doing important jobs despite the potential risk to their health.

To acknowledge what these workers were doing, people across the world displayed rainbows in their windows. Some sang from their balconies to spread joy to their communities even though they had to spend time apart.

When you drop a pebble into water, it creates a ripple that keeps spreading out. It's the same with showing kindness or appreciation: one good deed inspires another, meaning a single act can travel a long way.

Animal Helpers

These compassionate creatures prove it's not just humans who have the ability to be kind.

- Therapy dogs are specially trained to go into schools or hospitals where they help anxious children relax and cope with stress.

- Researchers have recorded Bonobo apes sharing treats with other bonobos, even ones they've never met.

- Humpback whales protect seals and other species from being attacked by killer whales.

killer whale

humpback whale

Elephants can use their trunks like arms. When one elephant is feeling upset, another member of the herd will give it a gentle stroke or trunk-hug.

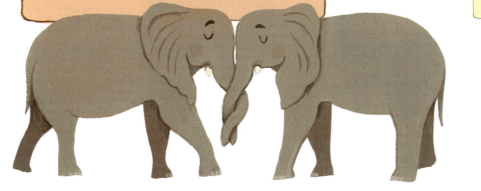

Now that you've discovered some wonderful ways to look after your wellbeing, it's time to put them into practice. Taking care of your mind and body helps you to feel fantastic and do your best.

Nobody feels great all the time because life is full of ups and downs, but that's even more reason to look after yourself. Remember, wellbeing isn't just for good days; it's for happy days, sad days, in-between days, holidays and every day. In fact, wellbeing is for life, so try to nurture it as well as you can.

Glossary

accessible: able to be reached easily; or be understood easily

adrenalin: a hormone that helps us respond to stressful situations

carnivores: animals that eat only meat

Covid-19: a fast-spreading virus that mainly affects people's ability to breathe; widely suffered during a pandemic beginning in 2019

herbivores: animals that eat only plants

hormone: chemicals produced in the body or in a plant that encourage growth or influence how the cells function

immune system: the body's system that helps keep us safe from disease

pandemic: a disease that spreads over a wide geographical area

psychologists: scientists who study the mind and how it works

REM (rapid eye movement): the dreaming stage of a sleep cycle

vulnerable: able to be hurt or harmed or attacked

welfare: the health and happiness of a person

Index

animals 20, 25, 27, 37, 39

appreciation 36

body 14–15, 18, 21–22, 25, 38–39

breathing 19, 28–29

chemicals 15, 25, 32, 39

circadian rhythm 21

Emmons, Dr Robert A 12

emotions 6–9, 25

empathy 33–34

fight or flight 27

food 4, 20, 22

gratitude 12–13

growth mindset 11

hormone 21, 26–27, 32, 39

kind 9, 24–25, 32, 37

positive 4, 10, 12, 15

resilience 5

sleep 17–21, 39

sport 11, 15–16

wellbeing 4–5, 10, 24–26, 28–29, 38

worries 9, 29–30